**ANIMALS**

in the wild

First published in Belgium and Holland by Clavis Uitgeverij, Hasselt – Amsterdam, 2015
Copyright © 2015, Clavis Uitgeverij

English translation from the Dutch by Clavis Publishing Inc. New York
Copyright © 2017 for the English language edition: Clavis Publishing Inc. New York

Visit us on the web at www.clavisbooks.com.

*Animals in the Wild. The Wolf* written and illustrated by Renne
Original title: *Wilde dieren in de natuur. De wolf*
Translated from the Dutch by Clavis Publishing

ISBN 978-1-60537-323-2

This book was printed in April 2017 at Publikum d.o.o., Slavka Rodica 6, Belgrade, Serbia

First Edition
10 9 8 7 6 5 4 3 2 1

Clavis Publishing supports the First Amendment and celebrates the right to read

# the
# WOLF

Renne

Clavis

**NEW YORK**

## WHERE DOES THE WOLF LIVE?

In the mountains and plains of the Northern Hemisphere,
a wonderful creature stalks through the woods. Oo-oo-oooo...!
Who is that, howling so mysteriously?
It's **the wolf**, a fascinating predator.

The wolf is an excellent hunter. He likes vast areas
with rippling streams, lush pants and tasty prey.

Wolves hunt in dense coniferous and deciduous forests,
steppes, grasslands and tundra. But they also feel at home
in the mountains. They love hunting mountain goats!

Something is stalking through the woods...

# WHAT DOES THE WOLF LOOK LIKE?

**The wolf** is a fast,
strong and intelligent canine.

His senses are very sharp –
not just his sight and hearing,
but also his **sense of smell**.

Look at those **teeth**!
His canines are at least 2 inches long!
You can see from his jaw that he is
a strong carnivore.

His **coat** is thick in winter
and thin in summer.
His fur is gray to reddish, but there
are white and black wolves too.

With his **long** and **muscular legs**,
he's a good runner.
The wolf can run long distances.
He can reach speeds of 30 miles
an hour!

Thanks to his **thick tail**, the wolf can keep his balance while running. The wolf also uses his tail to communicate with other wolves.

The wolf can't retract his **claws**. He doesn't use them to kill his prey either.

The wolf is a digitigrade. That means he walks on his toes and not on the pads of his feet.

# HOW DOES THE WOLF FILL HIS DAY?

Wolves are territorial: one pack defends a pretty large area.
Other wolves had better watch out:
They are not welcome here!

The wolf's territory is filled with prey: his food.
When hunting, the canines trot after one another, single file.
They can cover almost forty miles in twenty-four hours.
They are top athletes!
Wolves need water to drink, too. When the rivers are frozen,
wolves lick the snow or ice.

These are the wolf's **footprints**. Can you see that he has eight toes?

This is a tuft of hair from his **tail**!

Walking in a line...
Who will find prey first?

# HOW DO WOLVES LIVE TOGETHER?

The wolf lives in a group that's called a pack. He doesn't like to be alone!
A pack is formed by two adults and their young ones, so it's basically a family.
Most packs contain three to twenty wolves.
When more than one clan lives together, the packs can be bigger.
The strongest male and female are in charge of the pack. They are the dominant wolves.
The other wolves listen to them.
Wolves "talk" to each other by barking, growling or howling.
But they also use signs, like keeping their tail or ears up or down.

The **ears** and **tail** are **standing up** proudly to make the wolf look **taller**.

The ears are **flat** and the tail is **drawn in** to make the wolf look **smaller**.

**dominant wolf**                    **lower-ranking wolf**

Hey, you!
You'd better listen, or else...

# WHAT DOES THE WOLF EAT?

The wolf is a hunter. He can take down large prey such as fallow deer, goats or sheep. One wolf can take a reindeer, but a group of wolves can drive moose, musk deer and even bison into a corner. The wolf doesn't like to run after healthy animals. Sick or old animals are a lot easier to catch, so why wear himself out? If he can't find bigger prey, the wolf settles for small mammals, reptiles, frogs, birds, carrion or even fruit.

**Berries and fruit?**
The wolf eats them too.

The wolf's prey doesn't give up easily!

## WHAT'S THE WOLF'S SECRET?

For thousands of years a terrifying howl has echoed through the woods. How scary! It's the call of the wolf.

His mysterious howling has a function: when the other wolves hear it, they know that they have to come back, that it's time to go hunting together, or that there are other packs around.

You often hear their howling at the end of winter, when the mating season starts again. When the wolves are excited, they howl together.

Owoo-ooo-ooo!

Listen! The wolves are giving
a magical and mysterious concert.

# HOW DO WOLF CUBS COME INTO THIS WORLD?

Only the dominant couple in a pack has cubs. At the end of winter,
the alpha male and female are the only members of the pack who reproduce.
The she-wolf finds a natural hiding-place or makes a hole to have her cubs.
She has four to seven at a time.
The mother nurses her young. Later, when wolves are bigger,
she brings them meat. The father and the other wolves of the pack help her.

Wolves are good parents.
They take very good care of their cubs.
Little wolves that lose their parents
are often adopted.

**A ten-day-old cub**

**A three-month-old cub**

The hungry cubs fill their bellies!

## HOW DO WOLF CUBS GROW UP?

The cubs are well protected by the pack and grow up in safety.
Slowly but surely, they get to know the laws of the pack. They
find their place in the group by playing. When small wolves are
fully grown, they stay in the pack. They join in all activities and
help raise the new cubs.

Wait!
I'm coming!

Are we going to play? Come on!

# WHO DOES THE WOLF NEED TO WATCH OUT FOR?

The wolf only has one real enemy: man.
Man is terribly afraid of the wolf and tries to kill him out of fear.
Even worse, man intrudes on the wolf's natural habitat
by building roads and houses. That's why there is less
and less prey to eat and therefore there are fewer wolves.

Luckily this beautiful animal is protected in some areas.
There are wolf reserves in Italy, India, the United States
and other countries.

I'm safe here!

Hey...
where do I have
to go now?

# ONCE UPON A TIME...

In fairy tales, the wolf is always a cruel, scary and bloodthirsty animal.
Man has been afraid of the "big bad wolf" for ages, even though the wolf
would never attack a human being for no reason. On the contrary,
the wolf is afraid of humans and stays as far away from them as possible.

In ancient times, the wolf didn't have such a bad reputation.
The city of Rome, Italy, is said to have been founded by two "wolf children":
Romulus and Remus were adopted and raised by a she-wolf.
Later, the brothers founded the marvelous city that still exists today.

Roman coin with **Romulus** and **Remus**.

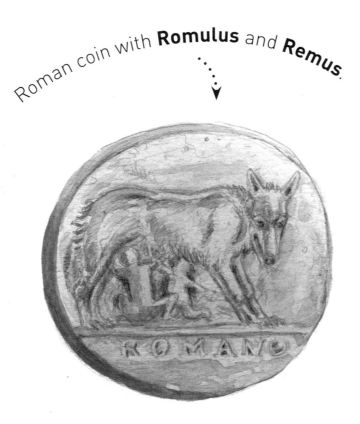

Little wolf,
where are you?

# THE FAMILY OF WOLVES

The wolf belongs to the family of canines.
This family includes 34 species. Canines live almost all over the world.
These are the types that are most common.

**Wolf:** Europe, Asia, North America
**African wild dog:** Africa
**Maned wolf:** South America
**Dog:** Europe, Africa, North and South America, Asia, Oceania
**Fox:** Europe, Africa, North America, Asia, Oceania
**Jackal:** Europe, Africa, Asia
**Coyote:** North America

**Dog**
*(Canis lupus familiaris)*

**Fox**
*(Vulpes vulpes)*

**Jackal**
*(Canis aureus)*

**Wolf**
*(Canis lupus)*

**African wild dog**
*(Lycaon pictus)*

**Maned wolf**
*(Chrysocyon brachyurus)*

**Coyote**
*(Canis latrans)*

# MORE FACTS ABOUT THE WOLF

**Class:** mammals

**Order:** predator

**Family:** canines

**Genus and species:** Canis lupus

**Total length:** up to 5 feet + tail (12 to 24 inches)

**Weight:** 90 to 180 pounds, depending on the region

**Habitat:** woods, mountains, tundra...

**Diet:** carnivor (deer, small mammals, reptiles, toads and frogs, birds, cattle, carrion, also berries and fruit)

**Lifestyle:** the wolf is social and lives in a pack of 3 to 20 animals

**Mating season:** end of winter

**Gestation:** about 2 months

**Birth of the wolf cubs:** spring

**Litter:** 4 to 7 cubs

**Sexually mature:** female at 2, male at 3

**Life expectancy:** about 10 years

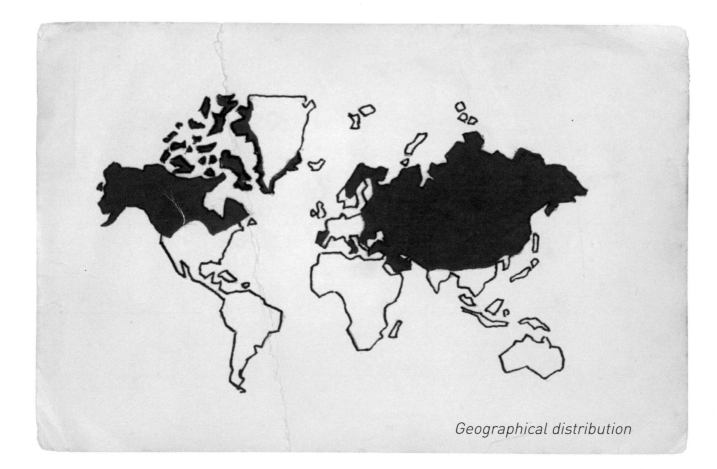

*Geographical distribution*

# NICE WORDS TO LEARN

- **HEMISPHERE:**
  one of the two halves of the earth, northern or southern

- **PREDATOR:**
  animal that hunts other animals for food

- **CARNIVORE:**
  animal that eats meat

- **DIGITIGRADE:**
  animal that touches the ground only with its toes while walking

- **TERRITORY:**
  area the animal lives in and defends

- **DOMINANT:**
  animal that is in command over other animals in a group

- **MATING SEASON:**
  time in which animals come together to make babies

- **MAMMALS:**
  animals that nurse their young

- **LITTER:**
  number of cubs an animal bears in one birth

- **LIFE EXPECTANCY:**
  normal duration of life